CW00327706

Some questions need answering more than once.

They hang around my life a lot of the time, by turns teasing me from the wings or challenging me centre stage. You think they've been settled and then, wow, they pop up again wearing different clothes. But underneath they're the same questions. They're the basics... things I need to wrestle with over and over again as I try to make sense of a world that's at once pretty wonderful and totally confusing.

It's all to do with identity. For a start, who am I? Me. Scientific reductions lay me out on a slab in terms of chemical compounds: I'm solids, liquids, gases. Psychological babble further classifies me - defines me in terms of neuroses, hormones, primitive instincts. Relationships pin me to a family tree: I'm his sister, their mother. And social structures compartmentalise me, too. I'm his neighbour, her colleague. Stripped of all that, in essence, who am I? And, maybe more intriguing, who was I meant to be?

Accepting that I am made to be in relationship, that my life really only makes sense as it is lived out with others, leads me on to further questions of identity. As I engage with these questions it is unavoidable - if I admit that a creation demands the existence of a creator - that I look at myself in the context of some bigger plan. God, it seems, is relational, too, for why else would he have reached across the huge divide from the divine to the human by sending his Son into the world to communicate himself to me? It seems I must tackle that other big question, the one about Jesus Christ: who is he? And if I identify myself with Jesus, say I believe in him, become adopted by God and therefore joined to his family, there are issues of how I fit into that family, known as the church. What and who are the church? How does it operate as community in the 21st century, and what will belonging mean for me?

Then there is the matter of the wider world. Within my birth family there are things which make me recognisably someone who belongs. Having grown up with them, I am used to their ways, I understand their jokes, and I share identifiable genetic likeness. I have my father's hair colour, traces of a regional accent. And within the family of the church, though incredibly disparate, there are common basics of faith, and perhaps shared expressions of faith.

But what of the many others with whom I struggle to find a trace of common ground? I scan the faces of the people in the airport arrivals lounge. Differences. Skin colour, language, social standing, customs, educational opportunity, morality, religious conviction, political viewpoint... so many important things on which I may feel 'other' to you. Who exactly are you, when you are different to me? And how should I relate to you?

This series of four booklets attempts to tap into the wisdom of God on some of these big questions that won't go away. What does the Bible say about who I am? About who Jesus really is? About the nature of the community of believers we call the church? About who you are when you are different to me?

You won't find all the answers here. But hopefully enough to get you started on discovering for yourself.

Lin Ball

Editor Lin Ball

Who am I ?

Bread for the Journey

Bread for the Journey

THE IDENTITY SERIES

Who am I?

Scripture taken from the Contemporary English
Version © American Bible Society, published by
HarperCollins Publishers, with kind permission
from the British and Foreign Bible Society.

British Library Cataloguing-in-Publication Data

A catalogue record for this book is available from
the British library.

Cover, internal design and print production by
CPO (Christian Publicity Organisation),
Garcia Estate, Canterbury Road, Worthing,
West Sussex, BN13 1BW.

First published 2001

ISBN 1 85999 504 7

*Understanding your word brings light
to the minds of ordinary people.*

Psalm 119:130

WITNESS @ WORK

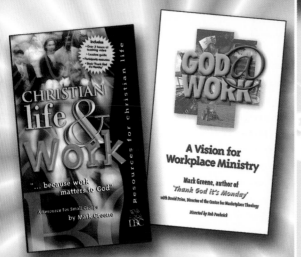

'THE MOST UNTAPPED OPPORTUNITY FOR EVANGELISM IS THE WORKPLACE'

Witness at work – but how?
Here's how...

ZX315 Christian Life & Work pack by Mark Greene

A six-part video, book and study guide pack, particularly for small groups, to help all who struggle with work-place issues as a Christian and to enhance our witness at work. Our lifestyle witnesses as much as our words. The video is presented by Mark Greene, Executive Director of the London Institute of Contemporary Christianity and former Vice Principal of London Bible College; the book and study guide are also written by Mark.
RRP: £25.00   CVC price: £20.00 (+ £4.00 p&p)
You save £5.00

ZX316V God@Work video

Two creative 20 minute programmes providing a stimulating Biblical introduction to God's view of work and an inspiring, practical vision for ministry and evangelism in the work-place. Fun, fast and full of stories. By Mark Greene, with David Prior, Director of the Centre for Marketplace Theology.
RRP: £12.99   CVC price: £11.99 (+ £4.00 p&p)
You save £1.00

ZX384 Christians@Work set

The Christian Life & Work pack plus the God@Work video.
RRP: £37.99   CVC price: £30.99 (+ £6.00 p&p)
You save £7.00

There are four titles in this *Bread for the Journey* series:

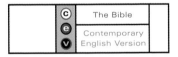

Who am I?

Who is He?

Who are we?

Who are you?

Each can be used on its own, individually or in a small group setting, or as part of a series. The material is arranged in a free-flowing way, moving between bite-sized chunks of selected Bible verses and comments.

Ⓒ	The Bible	
ⓔ	Contemporary	
Ⓥ	English Version	

The Bible verses are printed on the page, which makes the booklet self-contained. We've chosen the CEV (Contemporary English Version) because it's not only a translation that stands the test of good scholarship but it's readable and fresh. If you're new to Bible reading, it's a user-friendly version to begin with. If it's not a version you're familiar with, you may find it stimulating and helpful to read well-known verses put across in a new way. You can, of course, use any version of the Bible. You'll find the Bible references for each section given under the section headings, and Bible text is printed in italic.

The booklets are designed for reading straight through or for dipping into. You choose!

Extras: on your own or with others

It's a good idea to pray, even if it's just a couple of sentences, as you come to read. Ask God to speak to you through the material. Just the act of pausing in this way will help to focus your mind and still your heart to receive. Don't rush through the booklet. Even if you've only got a few minutes, read slowly and let the meaning sink in. If you've more time, here are a few suggestions which might make this opportunity to focus on God and his word more meaningful:

* As you read, rather than letting the words wash over you, ask yourself questions. What is this really saying? What is this showing me about God? What connection does this have with my own world, with my today?

* Keep a spiritual journal; note down things you learn about God; record fresh insights, anything you think God might be saying to you, prayer needs, answers to prayer.

* Think about how your time with God might involve some worship or expression of thankfulness. This could involve playing some praise music and singing along. Or expressing out loud your thanks to God. Or writing down your response, perhaps in a kind of 'love letter' to God.

* Listen for the voice of God! He very often chooses to speak directly to us through the Bible.

If you're part of a small fellowship that meets weekly or fortnightly, these booklets are great for working through together. Or you might like to get some friends together over coffee for a one-off discussion. You'll find a number of questions suitable for group discussion, and some prayer ideas, too, that would work well in a group.

Most of the ideas listed here could be adapted for small group use; or in pairs within a small group. Remember that God is a God of variety. He is creative and made us to be that way too. Don't be trapped into using formats simply because that's 'the way it's always done'. Use your group's creativity and imagination. Remember to value everyone's contribution. And think about other resources that might be useful in adding width and depth to the material - for example, a current film, novel or newspaper article that explores some of the themes of identity you will find in the series.

Who am I?

'And our next contestant is...'

Your adrenaline is pumping. The heat
from the glaring spotlights is making you
sweat. The TV quiz show host flourishes
the microphone under your nose and
you've got 30 seconds to tell the world
who you are. What do you say?

Well, who are you? Who am I?

Office worker? Mother? Mechanic? Trapeze artiste? But that's only what
<u>I do</u>... not what <u>I am.</u>

Forget the spotlights and the audience. Given a quiet corner and
a blank sheet of paper and all the time in the world... what would you
write down? Try making a list - real or in your head - but be prepared
for some crossings out and new thoughts as we look at some insights
from the Bible. You may well find some bigger - and probably
better - answers.

I am...

Who am I?

I am: a junior partner in the mission of Jesus to this world.

Wayne, friend, thinker, lover of sports and humour

I am: always available, always giving, always tired.

Megan, struggling to please, overworked, frustrated artist

I am: just another person, doing some half-crazy work for the Lord in Romania.

David, Archers fan

I am: a learner, grasping that the step of faith must reach from the reality of my present experience all the way to God's spectacular promises.

Mare, American, long-time missionary in Hong Kong

I am: becoming, which means that I have been shown the way onto God's ancient road, to meet Jesus in Jerusalem.

Allen, mid-career transition student and mountain-loving poet

I am: a husband, a father, an engineer... and an enigma!

Geoff, lover of how and why things work

I am: a creative, adventurous person, always looking for new and interesting things to do, and become involved in.

Colin, world traveller

I am: God's special child chosen to fulfil his purposes in the earth through my life.

Mary, health-conscious caregiver, home decorating buff

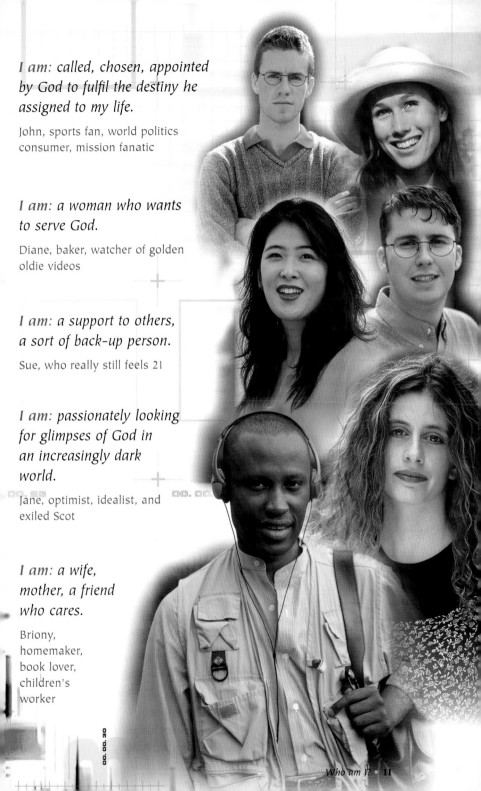

I am: called, chosen, appointed by God to fulfil the destiny he assigned to my life.

John, sports fan, world politics consumer, mission fanatic

I am: a woman who wants to serve God.

Diane, baker, watcher of golden oldie videos

I am: a support to others, a sort of back-up person.

Sue, who really still feels 21

I am: passionately looking for glimpses of God in an increasingly dark world.

Jane, optimist, idealist, and exiled Scot

I am: a wife, mother, a friend who cares.

Briony, homemaker, book lover, children's worker

I am: made by God

Genesis 1:26-31

God said, *"Now we will make humans, and they will be like us. We will let them rule the fish, the birds, and all other living creatures."*

So God created humans to be like himself; he made men and women. God gave them his blessing and said:

"Have a lot of children! Fill the earth with people and bring it under your control. Rule over the fish in the sea, the birds in the sky, and every animal on the earth.

"I have provided all kinds of fruit and grain for you to eat. And I have given the green plants as food for everything else that breathes. These will be food for animals, both wild and tame, and for birds."

I didn't bring myself into being. My parents played their part, but it was God who chose to give me existence. Like the rest of creation, I am totally dependent on him for having life and for continuing life. I am - and it's God who should be thanked for that!

Not only did God make us but - and this is truly amazing! - God makes us to be *like himself*. Or as the Bible passage puts it, *like us*. It's worth remembering that he's the God of a loving family relationship - Father, Son and Holy Spirit. In his likeness, we're made for relationship - with him, with the world around us, with one another. He is our heavenly father; we are his children. And it's within the context of these love relationships that we have children of our own and take charge of the world we live in. We're not on the earth to exploit either the environment or each other. Rape and robbery is not God's will. If we're *like God*, we should learn to behave like him. But, let's be honest... do we feel at all like God? Can we even say we know what God is really like?

God looked
at what he had done.
All of it was very good!

Everything God had created was - like God himself - very good. That much we know - and maybe not a lot more. But it's important to find out. Who am I? God's child, made in his image. But what does that mean? Who is God and what is he like? Where can I look in a mirror and see his undistorted image instead of the blur that is my day-to-day self?

I am: known completely by God, guided and protected by him

Psalm 139:1-12

You have looked deep into my heart, Lord,
and you know all about me.

You know when I am resting or when I am working,
and from heaven you discover my thoughts.

You notice everything I do and
everywhere I go.

Before I even speak a word,
you know what I will say,

and with your powerful arm
you protect me from every side.

I can't understand all this!
Such wonderful knowledge is far
above me.

David, who wrote this psalm, is aware that God is with him at every moment. It's not a *Big Brother* situation. He's not scared to look up in case his face or behaviour is caught on camera. He's aware of God's presence, is reassured by God's intimate knowledge of him, and sees that relationship as something marvellous.

Where could I go to escape
  from your Spirit or from your sight?

If I were to climb up to the highest heavens,
  you would be there.

If I were to dig down to the world of the dead
  you would also be there.

Suppose I had wings like the dawning day
  and flew across the ocean.

Even then your powerful arm
  would guide and protect me.

Or suppose I said, "I'll hide in the dark
  until night comes to cover me over."

But you see in the dark
  because daylight and dark are all the
  same to you.

God's for-always presence is protecting,
helpful. There are no dark corners from
God's perspective. Everywhere is light.

I am: put together by God from the beginning of life

Psalm 139:13-16

You are the one who put me together
*   inside my mother's body,*

and I praise you
*   because of the wonderful way you created me.*

Everything you do is marvellous!

*   Of this I have no doubt.*

Nothing about me is hidden from you!

I was secretly woven together
*   deep in the earth below,*

but with your own eyes
*   you saw my body being formed.*

Even before I was born, you had written in your book
*   everything I would do.*

God has created me and cared for me from the moment of conception. He knows everything about each one of us - even how and when things will go wrong - and he treats us with love and respect.

Does knowing this shape my own sense of self-worth? Shape the respect I have for others?

Tell me...

'This world is a great sculptor's shop. We are the statues and there is a rumour going round the shop that some of us are some day going to come to life!'

C S Lewis, theologian, in his book *Mere Christianity*

I am: hungry!

Genesis 3:1-7 / John 6:35

Hungry! So was the woman in the garden.
The story of the snake tempting Eve is well-known.
Even more well-known is the experience of
being tempted that the story describes.

The snake was more

cunning than any of the

other wild animals that the

Lord God had made. One day

it came to the woman and

asked, "Did God tell you not to

eat fruit from any tree in the garden?"

The woman answered, "God said we could eat fruit from any

tree in the garden, except the one in the middle. He told us

not to eat fruit from that tree or even to touch it. If we do,

we will die."

"No, you won't!" the snake replied.

"God understands what will

happen on the day you eat

fruit from that tree. You

will see what you have

done, and you will know the difference between right and wrong, just as God does."

The woman stared at the fruit. It looked beautiful and tasty. She wanted the wisdom that it would give her, and she ate some of the fruit. Her husband was there with her, so she gave some to him, and he ate it too. Straight away they saw what they had done, and they realized they were naked. Then they sewed fig leaves together to make something to cover themselves.

Hunger is natural. We're designed that way - not just to long
for food, but for companionship, for all kinds of satisfactions. And we have a deep longing to know God and to know God's wisdom.

We also have a frightening amount of self-will. Like Eve, so often we mis-direct our good hunger pangs. We develop greed, cravings that go against God's will for us. We find we are hungry for power, for flattery, for self-sufficiency apart from God.

When my daughter was a toddler, she said one day, 'I'm hungry.' So I offered her some bread and butter. She pushed it away. 'No! I'm hungry for sweets.'

How often do we push away the spiritually nourishing things that God wants to give us, because our eyes have seen something that seems more attractive?

I am: hungry. But is my hunger real? I am: self-willed. I have blunted my hunger for God and directed it towards selfishness. I am: a distorted image of God. How can I satisfy my hunger in the way God intended?

Jesus replied: "I am the bread that gives life! No one who comes to me will ever be hungry. No one who has faith in me will ever be thirsty."

I am: hungry to know you, to know myself

Exodus 3:14,15

God said to Moses: "I am the eternal God. So tell them that the Lord, whose name is 'I Am', has sent you. This is my name for ever, and it is the name that people must use from now on."

When Moses asks God his name, he's looking for a definition. Not just to know who this God is, but also to know what this God is for. Is he the god of the sun or the moon, of good harvests or safe journeys?

God doesn't have that sort of name. He isn't this god or that god, with one function among many. He simply is. 'I am'. He can't be limited by definitions.

God is. He exists - and that fact should fill us with such gratitude that we don't need to question him further.

But, being human, we do. Constantly. 'Who are you, Lord?' God just replies, 'I am'.

Who am I? God has told me I am made in his image. But sin has obscured that image. So where can I see God's image and know what my true identity is?

Can you pray these words? Lord, how thankful I am for just being. How thankful I am for being me - unique, and cherished by you. Father, it is my deepest desire to know you more fully, and so to truly know myself. I am hungry to know you, and in you to know and love all you have created. Amen.

I am: following Jesus, the way

John 14:6

"I am the way, the truth, and the life!" Jesus answered.

"Without me, no one can go to the Father."

Look at me! Jesus says to each one of us. Since the day Eve sinned we've lost the chance of looking into the mirror and seeing God in ourselves. But we can look in the Gospels and see God in Jesus - see exactly what it's possible for a human being to be. Try dipping into the fifth chapter of Matthew, where Jesus describes the way to live a life of selfless love, or the fifth chapter of Mark, where he puts his love into practice by healing people.

The more we look at Jesus, the more we discover our real potential.

I am: capable of changing
direction

Acts 26:9–20

Scripture Union

Bread for the Journey

Please give us your reaction

We would like to hear from you. In the centre of this insert is a
questionnaire and we'd really appreciate it if you would feed back to us
your thoughts on this publication. Once you have completed the
questionnaire, please remove the whole sheet, fold along the dotted lines,
tuck one flap into the other, ensuring the FREEPOST address panel appears
on the outside. Then drop it into your nearest post box.

**Scripture Union is a registered charity (No. 213422) and if you would
like to save us the postage cost, please use a 2nd class stamp.**

Thank you for sparing a few moments

to complete this questionnaire. We want to ensure that Bible reading and study programmes are tailored to the needs of users and your response will be invaluable in helping us to plan and shape future publications.

Once you have completed the questionnaire, please fold along the dotted lines on the reverse side, tuck one flap into the other and post to us at Scripture Union.

---

①
Please tick the title you have been using.

Who am I? ☐   Who is He? ☐
Who are we? ☐   Who are you? ☐

②
How did you come into contact with Bread for the Journey series? (please tick one box)

☐ Advertisement in the Christian press
☐ Article in the Christian press
☐ Through Scripture Union Bible reading notes
☐ Information at an exhibition/event
☐ Recommended by a friend
☐ Announcement at church
☐ Saw in a Christian bookshop
☐ Received as a gift
Other [＿＿＿＿＿＿＿＿＿＿＿]

③
What persuaded you to try Bread for the Journey? (please tick the boxes that apply)

☐ Cover design
☐ Title
☐ Content looked interesting
☐ Undated nature of the sections
☐ Price
☐ Subject and theme
☐ Scripture Union publication
☐ Prefer to read the Bible at own pace
☐ Quality of writing
☐ Design and layout
☐ Size of book
☐ Wanted to transfer from SU dated notes
Other [＿＿＿＿＿＿＿＿＿＿＿]

④
How did you find the use of Bread for the Journey? (please tick one box)

Very easy ☐ Fairly easy ☐ Neither easy nor difficult ☐ Fairly difficult ☐
Very difficult ☐

⑤
What did you like about Bread for the Journey?

[＿＿＿＿＿＿＿＿＿＿＿＿＿＿]

⑥
What did you dislike about Bread for the Journey?

[＿＿＿＿＿＿＿＿＿＿＿＿＿＿]

⑦
What other topics and themes would you like covered in Bread for the Journey series?

[＿＿＿＿＿＿＿＿＿＿＿＿＿＿]

8

The way people read the Bible varies widely across the country as do people's experiences of God speaking to them through his word. It would help us to know how you normally use the Bible. (Please tick the boxes that apply)

	Using Scripture Union notes (Please say which)	Using undated explanatory notes (Please give title)	Using other Bible aids (Please specify)	Prefer not to use notes
Daily reading				
Monday to Friday				
2 or 3 times a week				
Weekends				
Regularly but no pattern				
Irregularly				
Use Sunday sermon as a starting point for study				
Other pattern				

9

Your details

Name _____

Address _____

_____

Postcode _____

Church name and location (if applicable) _____

Your age profile (optional)

Under 18 ☐ 18-30 ☐ 31-40 ☐ 41-50 ☐ 51-60 ☐ 61-65 ☐ over 65 ☐

Position in church (tick those applicable)

Member ☐ Housegroup leader ☐ Church leader/minister ☐ Elder ☐ Deacon ☐

Lay reader ☐ Pastoral assistant ☐ Youth leader ☐ Children's leader ☐ Missions

representative ☐ Prayer co-ordinator ☐ Other _____

Thank you for taking the time to complete this questionnaire.

fold first

This is a
FREEPOST
mailer but if you
affix a 2nd class
stamp it will
help support
Scripture Union

Scripture Union
Bible Ministries Publishing
FREEPOST ANG5570
Milton Keynes
MK2 2YR

second fold

Tuck one flap into the other to
form folded mailer

New Testament writer

Paul gives a vivid picture of how it's possible to make a complete turnabout in life. He describes how he was full of hatred for the Christians and for what - or who - they stood for: Jesus of Nazareth. Like fanatics in every age, Paul ended up committing atrocities in the name of what he - not God - decided was a 'just cause'.

I once thought that I should do everything I could to oppose Jesus from Nazareth. I did this first in Jerusalem, and with the authority of the chief priests I put many of God's people in jail.

I even voted for them to be killed.

I often had them punished in our meeting places, and I tried to make them give up their faith.

In fact, I was so angry with them, that I went looking for them in foreign cities.

But God had other plans for him, and confronts him in a direct and frightening way.

... one day I was on my way to Damascus with the authority and permission of the chief priests. About midday I saw a light brighter than the sun. It flashed from heaven on me and on everyone travelling with me. We all fell to the ground. Then I heard a voice say to me in Aramaic, "Saul, Saul, why are you so cruel to me? It's foolish to fight against me!"

"Who are you?" I asked.

Then the Lord answered, "I am Jesus! I am the one you are so cruel to."

The response, *I am Jesus*, must have been devastating to Paul.

Jesus! The dead and buried charlatan - so Paul thinks - whose followers had to be crushed at all costs! Can we begin to imagine how his heart must have thumped? He'd given his life to the cause of fighting this imposter, and here he is, alive, and calling him to be his follower.

"Now stand up. I have appeared to you, because I have chosen you to be my servant. You are to tell others what you have learnt about me and what I will show you later."

The Lord also said, "I will protect you from the Jews and from the

Gentiles that I am sending you to. I want you to open their eyes, so that they will turn from darkness to light and from the power of Satan to God. Then their sins will be forgiven, and by faith in me they will become part of God's holy people."

Christ reveals not only who he is and something of his power - as if Paul now had any doubt! - but also the new cause to which Paul must give his life. Jesus has come to him as a light - literally a blinding light, because for some days Paul was to lose his sight - for the purpose of sending Paul to bring God's light to other people.

... I obeyed this vision from heaven. First I preached to the people in Damascus, and then I went to Jerusalem and all over Judea. Finally, I went to the Gentiles and said, "Stop sinning and turn to God! Then prove what you have done by the way you live."

Paul says 'yes' to Jesus and becomes a new person. The rest of his life is living proof to that change.

A striking story. Are you tempted to think that it's just a one-off? That such dramatic changes don't happen nowadays?

A young man,
aggressively atheist, was one evening suddenly confronted by the presence of Christ standing by his desk. The next morning, as he left home and looked around at the people in the street, he was overcome by the fact that the God he now knew existed and loved him, must love every one of these strangers, too. He decided there and then to spend the rest of his life bringing the good news of God's existence and God's love to people. I heard this story from his own lips after he'd spent 50 years in the service of God.

Tell me...
'If you were arrested for being a Christian, would there be enough evidence to convict you?'
David Otis Fuller

Meet our writer Gillian

'Don't say you can't start at the top!' says Gillian Crow. Her writing career began by submitting her first article - on the resurrection - to the Times newspaper. Since then she's written many articles on religion for the national and the Christian press, as well as some religious educational material, travel articles and poetry.

A few years ago Gillian had her first book published: *Grains of Salt and Rays of Light - reflections on St. Matthew's Gospel*. She is also half-way through a novel. Writing about her faith has led to quite a few speaking engagements. Her career has also included some periods in the civil service, counselling with the Department of Employment, and helping her husband in his management consultancy business. Travel, classical music and swimming are all on her list of favourite things to do.

Gillian, did you have a religious background? How have your ideas about your own identity developed?

I was born in London into an agnostic family, although I developed a very firm belief in God in my childhood. But I didn't start going to church until my late teens. And it was some time later that I was received into the Russian Orthodox Church.

I can remember as a child having a very strong idea about my own identity. Then, after I married and had children, I began to think of myself more and more in terms of being someone's wife, someone's mother... it took me a long time to realise that human love can be demanding and even devouring, so that you can become just an adjunct of another person. And later I came to see how very different this is from God's love for us. In the light of God's love we become not less of a person but more. We expand. We grow. And I find this exciting, because as you get older you think you're not capable of growing any more, in day-to-day-terms, whereas in Jesus' terms you go on growing all the time.

What do you think are the confusions about identity that people most struggle with?

Well, I think a lot of people do confuse what they do for a living with what they are. And, unfortunately, those who come to realise this isn't right, but don't know God, tend to get even more confused by New Age-type ideas such as 'Learn to get in touch with your inner self' when that inner self is described as a purely internal thing, with no reference to God. And that sort of inwardness, and all the associated ideas of holistic living, are okay so long as things as going well. But, when the going gets tough - well, our own inner strength and resources are really so small, compared with the greatness of God and what he offers us. Let's face it, if we don't realise that our true identity is being a child of God, then we're floundering.

How do you try to achieve and maintain a healthy self-image?

By coming back again and again to the Gospel, to prayer, to the realisation that I am loved by God. In my own life, people have let me down badly. I've been humiliated and made to feel worthless. So I have to take that to God and rediscover the fact that he thinks I'm worth dying for - not in theory, but that it has really happened. In general terms, God has thought humanity worth so much that he has become one of us! And then he comes to each of us and whispers the individual message: you're worth my life. That's pretty stupendous - so stupendous I think we sometimes think of it in too distant a way! You know the idea of standing in front of the mirror each day and repeating: every day and in every way, I am getting better and better. Well, Christians can stand in front of the mirror and say truthfully each morning: I am made in the image of God himself! And every day when we read the Gospel we can look at the image of Jesus described there and know that's meant to be OUR true self-image, something positive to work towards in the power of the Holy Spirit.

> God has thought humanity worth so much that he has become one of us!

Was there anything particular that challenged you as you wrote Who am I?

Yes, the vastness of the whole subject! It can't all be said, even begin to be said, in a short publication. I knew before I started that who I am depends in the first place on who God is - but the more you think about it, the deeper and richer that idea becomes. I could see how so many things tied up - the 'I am' of the God of Exodus, the 'I am' sayings of Jesus - and all tied up with who I am as a human person. As I was writing

there was all the talk in the media about the mapping of the human genome, which tells us who we are according to the particular scientific perspective - but nothing about us as real live people! So, yes, the vastness.

What one thing would you say people need to appreciate about being human today?

That our humanity is God-given, and therefore has the potential to be good. I don't like to hear people saying 'we're only human' as an excuse for bad things. I remember hearing a beautiful sermon in which the preacher summed up the parable of the sheep and the goats by saying that all God will ask us at the Last Judgement is: have you been truly human - in Christ's terms? The Bible is not just a book of wise sayings and commandments. It actually tells how one Man led a perfect life, and gives us his words: follow me. That's what being human is really about.

How do you think having a right view of who we are makes for a right view of who God is?

I think it's the other way round! I don't think we can really begin to understand our true potential, and have a right view of who we are, if we don't have a right view - or any view - of God. The atheist will never get it right. The fact is, because of our fallenness, our sinfulness, we're all sick. We can't see straight. We can't cure ourselves. It's only through God that we can be made whole. The New Age has got it right in a sense - yes, wholeness is vital. But we can't be made whole so long as we stop God from making us whole. How can I know who I am if I don't know that God has made me and died for me?

I am: on my way home

Luke 15:17-24

Do you remember the story of the young man we call the Prodigal Son? He went off with his share of the family inheritance, ran through it in no time, and ended up on the scrap heap. We pick up the action at its turning point.

... he came to his senses and said, "My father's workers have plenty to eat, and here I am, starving to death! I will go to my father and say to him, 'Father, I have sinned against God in heaven and against you. I am no longer good enough to be called your son. Treat me like one of your workers.' "

Sometimes it's only when we hit rock bottom that we're capable of a change of heart. The son knows that unless he returns home he has no hope. He knows he's blown it with his father - and he's blown it with God, too. He's lived such a bad life that he's destroyed his personal relationship with both. He's no longer his father's child - or God's. But maybe, just maybe, he can come back as an outsider, a worker who'll get his wages but won't share in the love that a child would expect. He can't say, 'Who am I? - A son'. So he'll settle for 'What am I? - a worker'.

The younger son got up and started back to his father. But when he was still a long way off, his father saw him and felt sorry for him. He ran to his son and hugged and kissed him.

The son said, "Father, I have sinned against God in heaven and against you. I am no longer good enough to be called your son."

We might guess what the father's answer will be! He's been watching with an aching heart for the return of the child he loves. He's not angry. He's sorry for this bedraggled specimen who appears in the distance; he's full of hugs and kisses as he runs to meet him. He gives him the chance to pour out his anguish and sorrow. But...

But his father said to the servants, "Hurry and bring the best clothes and put them on him. Give him a ring for his finger and sandals for his feet. Get the best calf and prepare it, so we can eat and celebrate. This son of mine was dead, but has now come back to life. He was lost and has now been found." And they began to celebrate.

Does he want his son to be reduced to being just a paid worker? He stops the lad before he can get the words out. He's not a *what*. He's a *who*. A very

special who. His son! The son who has returned home, returned to life. The father shows his son the truth about himself: who he really is.

Jesus wants this story to be my story and your story - today. The father is God, and the son is every single one of us who wants and needs to go home. Whenever we lose our way in life, whenever we're tempted to define ourselves as *what* and not *who*, God calls us back to remind us we're his children, and that our brother Jesus is the way, the truth and the life that makes this possible.

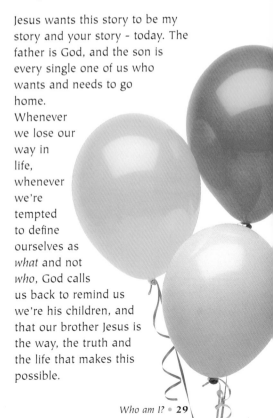

I am: a sheep in need and a shepherd in training

John 10:11-14

"I am the good shepherd, and the good shepherd gives up his life for his sheep. Hired workers are not like the shepherd. They don't own the sheep, and when they see a wolf coming, they run off and leave the sheep. Then the wolf attacks and scatters the flock. Hired workers run away because they don't care about the sheep.

I am the good shepherd. I know my sheep, and they know me."

Perhaps you're wondering: What's wrong with being a worker? Doing a job well and getting paid for it?

It's not a love relationship. Jesus loves his flock so much that he is willing to give his life for each sheep. Hired workers don't do that, he says. It's just not in their contract. As Jesus talks of the shepherd willingly giving his life, these are not empty words. He knows it won't be long before he's hanging on a cross in agony, proving his love.

There are two pictures to take in here: firstly, that I am part of Christ's flock, enfolded in a love that knows no bounds. And secondly, that I am to be like him - not limiting my giving to that of the hired worker, but learning to be a fellow shepherd, ready to give myself 100 per cent for the sheep.

I am: as much a sinner as the next person

Romans 2:1-11

Some of you accuse others of doing wrong. But there is no excuse for what you do. When you judge others, you condemn yourselves, because you are guilty of doing the very same things. We know that God is right to judge everyone who behaves in this way. Do you really think God won't punish you, when you behave exactly like the people you accuse? You don't think much of God's wonderful goodness or of his patience and willingness to put up with you. Don't you know that the reason God is good to you is because he wants you to turn to him?

It's so easy to see other people's faults and even easier to condemn them! But aren't I just as bad? Maybe I don't feel God is condemning me. Not today. Fair enough. But Paul reminds us we must understand why that is: God is patiently waiting for us to return to him.

But you are stubborn and refuse to turn to God. So you are making things even worse for yourselves on that day when he will show how angry he is and will judge the world with fairness. God will reward each of us for what we have done. He will give eternal life to everyone who has patiently done what is good in the hope of receiving glory, honour, and life that lasts for ever. But he will show how angry and furious he can be with every selfish person who rejects the truth and wants to do evil.

God's judgement will be fair with the sort of fairness that we long for with regard to others - but maybe I'd prefer mercy to justice for myself! I am: made for eternal life, that is, to share in the life of the eternal God. But that's impossible if I remain hostile to his goodness and forgiveness.

All who are wicked will be punished with trouble and suffering. It doesn't matter if they are Jews or Gentiles. But all who do right will be rewarded with glory, honour, and peace, whether they are Jews or Gentiles. God doesn't have any favourites!

And that goes for everyone. We've all missed the mark in God's eyes. We can't claim exemption because of what we are - only because of who we are: new people in Christ.

I am: forgiven

Matthew 18:21-35

We can't be new people and become like Jesus unless we feel the warmth of his forgiveness.

Peter came up to the Lord and asked, "How many times should I forgive someone who does something wrong to me? Is seven times enough?"

Jesus answered:

"Not just seven times, but seventy-seven times! This story will show you what the kingdom of heaven is like: One day a king decided to call in his officials and ask them to give an account of what they owed him. As he was doing this, one official was brought in who owed him fifty million silver coins. But he didn't have any money to pay what he owed. The king ordered him to be sold, along with his wife and children and all he owned, in order to pay the debt.

The official got down on his knees and began begging, "Have pity on me, and I will pay you every penny I owe!" The king felt sorry for him and let him go free. He even told the official that he did not have to pay back the money."

The official certainly

wanted mercy, not justice. Don't we all promise a change of heart like him when we're desperate?

Now for the rest of the story.

As the official was leaving, he happened to meet another official, who owed him a hundred silver coins. So he grabbed the man by the throat. He started choking him and said, "Pay me what you owe!"

The man got down on his knees and began begging, "Have pity on me, and I will pay you back." But the first official refused to have pity. Instead, he went and had the other official put in jail until he could pay what he owed.

When some other officials found out what had happened, they felt sorry for the man who had been put in jail. Then they told the king what had happened. The king called the first official back in and said, "You're an evil man! When you begged for mercy, I said you did not have to pay back a penny. Don't you think you should show pity to someone else, as I did to you?" The king was so angry that he ordered the official to be tortured until he could pay back everything he owed. That is how my Father in heaven will treat you, if you don't forgive each of my followers with all your heart.

We can be assured that God will forgive us if we're sorry and mean to change. When we have accepted God's forgiveness we can start again in a new restored relationship with him, our slates wiped clean. But in this new relationship with God, we should see things from his viewpoint.

I am: chosen by God

Ephesians 1:3-11

Praise the God and Father of our Lord Jesus Christ for the spiritual blessings that Christ has brought us from heaven! Before the world was created, God had Christ choose us to live with him and to be his holy and innocent and loving people.

Remember how it feels when you first fall in love? The sheer amazement that someone else has given their heart to you, of all the people in the world? Suddenly, you have a new purpose: to love and to bring joy to your soul-mate! And then, those of us that are parents... can you remember that rush of love you felt when you held your newborn son or daughter?

God was kind and decided that Christ would choose us to be God's own adopted children.

That's how God feels about us! We've become adopted sons and daughters, brothers and sisters of Christ.

God was very kind to us because of the Son he dearly loves, and so we should praise God.

Christ sacrificed his life's blood to set us free, which means that our sins are now forgiven. Christ did this because God was so kind to us. God has great wisdom and understanding, and by what Christ has done, God has shown us his own mysterious ways.

But what will it cost the family to take in these adopted children? God has weighed this up, too. In order to adopt us, he has had to sacrifice nothing less than the life-blood of his own son! It is part of his plan to save us from separation from him. And Jesus, sharing his Father's love for us, makes the sacrifice willingly.

Then when the time is right, God will do all that he has planned, and Christ will bring together everything in heaven and on earth.

God always does what he plans, and that's why he appointed Christ to choose us.

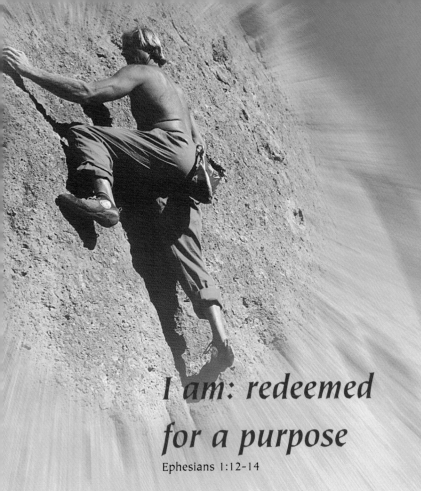

I am: redeemed
for a purpose

Ephesians 1:12-14

We've heard from Paul about his changed life - and the new purpose
for his life. But Paul tells us that we are all part of God's wonderful
plan for the world.

*He did this so that we Jews would bring honour to him and be the first ones
to have hope because of him. Christ also brought you the truth, which is the
good news about how you can be saved. You put your faith in Christ and
were given the promised Holy Spirit to show that you belong to God. The
Spirit also makes us sure that we will be given what God has stored up for his
people. Then we will be set free, and God will be honoured and praised.*

God's purpose is to give us hope, truth and freedom. And not in some
abstract way. We've been given the Holy Spirit himself as proof that we
belong to God. Read this bit again: *Christ will bring together everything in
heaven and on earth.* Yes, <u>we</u> are part of God's plan to bring heaven and
earth together - as we live as Christ's likenesses.

I am: alive with God's Spirit

Romans 8:1-8

If you belong to Christ Jesus, *you won't be punished. The Holy Spirit will give you life that comes from Christ Jesus and will set you free from sin and death. The Law of Moses cannot do this, because our selfish desires make the Law weak. But God set you free when he sent his own Son to be like us sinners and to be a sacrifice for our sin. God used Christ's body to condemn sin. He did this, so that we would do what the Law commands by obeying the Spirit instead of our own desires.*

We just can't live up to being new people in Christ unless we keep ourselves open to the Holy spirit. Only by letting the Spirit guide us will we be capable of doing God's will.

People who are ruled by their desires think only of themselves. Everyone who is ruled by the Holy Spirit thinks about spiritual things. If our minds are ruled by our desires, we will die. But if our minds are ruled by the Spirit, we will have life and peace. Our desires fight against God, because they do not and cannot obey God's laws. If we follow our desires, we cannot please God.

Otherwise, we'll continue to 'do our own thing' - and be as distant from God as ever!

I am: not a slave
– but a child of God

Romans 8:9-16 / Galatians 4:6-9

You are no longer ruled *by your desires, but by God's Spirit, who lives in you. People who don't have the Spirit of Christ in them don't belong to him. But Christ lives in you. So you are alive because God has accepted you, even though your bodies must die because of your sins. Yet God raised Jesus to life! God's Spirit now lives in you, and he will raise you to life by his Spirit.*

My dear friends, we must not live to satisfy our desires. If you do, you will die. But you will live, if by the help of God's Spirit you say 'No' to your desires.

Do I say 'yes' to self-will and death? Or 'yes' to Christ and life?

Only those people who are led by God's Spirit are his children. God's Spirit doesn't make us slaves who are afraid of him. Instead, we become his children and call him our Father. God's Spirit makes us sure that we are his children.

People have often said to me, 'Aren't you like your father!' If we are God's children, then we should be recognisably like him.

Now that we are his children, God has sent the Spirit of his Son into our hearts. And his Spirit tells us that God is our Father. You are no longer slaves. You are God's children, and you will be given what he has promised.

Before you knew God, you were slaves of gods that are not real. But now you know God, or better still, God knows you. How can you turn back and become the slaves of those weak and pitiful powers?

The Bible is a mirror in which I can discover my true likeness. How like my Father God am I? Do I carry the marks of slavery or true freedom?

I am: king and priest

Revelation 5:9,10

Read this lyric from the song to Jesus being sung in John's vision of the end of the world:

And with your own blood

you bought for God

people from every tribe,

language, nation and race.

You let them become kings

and serve God as priests,

and they will rule on earth.

And please read 'kings <u>and</u> queens'!

You could say this brings us right back to the beginning, to those verses in Genesis where God creates us to rule the earth. The plan went wrong because of our sin - but one day it will be reinstated. The one perfect ruler and priest is Jesus himself. But he has chosen us to become a living part of his work. Christians share in the priesthood of Christ, empowered through following him. And all this is possible because <u>I am: loved by the God who is himself Love.</u>

Father, I love you because you first loved me and you continue to love me. I ask for the power of the Holy Spirit to fill me and be at work in me every day, showing your love to others.

I am:

essential to the health of my world

Matthew 5:13-16

You are like salt for everyone on earth. But if salt no longer tastes like salt, how can it make food salty? All it is good for is to be thrown out and walked on.

You are like light for the whole world. A city built on top of a hill cannot be hidden, and no one would light a lamp and put it under a clay pot. A lamp is placed on a lampstand, where it can give light to everyone in the house. Make your light shine, so that others will see the good that you do and will praise your Father in heaven.

You're going on a picnic. The sun is shining. You've prepared a delicious spread. And you know the ideal spot...

What happens? You get stuck in slow-moving traffic. By the time you get there, grey clouds have obscured the sun and it's started to rain. Quick, back in the car, everyone! You ferret in the back for the lovely salad and cold meats. And bother! You've forgotten to bring the salt... and the pepper... and the salad

dressing! Instead of an idyllic day and a lunch fit for a king, the weather's dark, wet and miserable and the food tasteless.

But Jesus isn't talking about a spoilt picnic here. Salt and light aren't merely extras in the scenes he pictures. They are two things the world's eco-system just can't do without. We're talking about a planet in eternal darkness, incapable of sustaining life.

Jesus says that unless his followers bring God's spiritual salt and light to the world, there will be nothing but the bitterness of evil and the darkness of despair.

We're that important in God's plan. What an incredible thought! God values us so highly... and wants us to live up to nothing but the very best.

Father, your desire is for me to be salt and light to the earth. You have chosen me to be the world's life-giving, life-cleansing, life-enriching qualities. How wonderful! How grateful I should be that you have put such trust in me. Help me to be more aware of your presence and your power to enable me to fulfil your will for me and the world. Amen.

I am: a sharer in God's goodness

2 Peter 1:3-11

It's easy to make excuses. Circumstances, we claim, prevent us from being the image of God. But look at what Peter says here: we have everything we need!

We have everything we need to live a life that pleases God. It was all given to us by God's own power, when we learnt that he had invited us to share in his wonderful goodness. God made great and marvellous promises, so that his nature would become part of us. Then we could escape our evil desires and the corrupt influences of this world.

Do your best to improve your faith. You can do this by adding goodness, understanding, self-control, patience, devotion to God, concern for others, and love. If you keep

growing in this way, it will show that what you know about our Lord Jesus Christ has made your lives useful and meaningful. But if you don't grow, you are like someone who is nearsighted or blind, and you have forgotten that your past sins are forgiven.

My friends, you must do all you can to show that God has really chosen and selected you. If you keep on doing this, you won't stumble and fall. Then our Lord and Saviour Jesus Christ will give you a glorious welcome into his kingdom that will last for ever.

Not only are we invited to share God's goodness, but he's promised that his very nature will become part of us. And Peter gives us a checklist of qualities against which to measure ourselves. Look back at the verses again. Am I good, understanding, patient, devoted to God, concerned for others... Does this description ring true of me?

Peter encourages us to work towards this. We must be able to show others that when they want to know who God is, they can look at us and see that...

I am: the image of I AM

SLICED, GRANARY, WHOLEMEAL...

Bread comes in lots of different shapes, sizes and tastes. If you've liked the taste of *Bread for the Journey* we hope you'll look out for more titles under that series heading and get spiritually well-nourished.

But Scripture Union publishes a great many other titles that aim to open up the Bible to people of different tastes.

Another series you might like to try is *DAYZD*. The four titles in the *DAYZD* series cover Relationships, Guidance, Evangelism and Worship. Each gives 90 days undated Bible readings - eternal values presented in an up-to-the-minute style.

Then there's *DAILY BREAD* - a quarterly publication giving practical daily comments

relating the Bible to everyday life. Special features include information panels to give a deeper understanding of the Bible and a 'Talkabout' section with questions to use personally or in a small group.

And *CLOSER TO GOD*. Also quarterly, the special emphasis of this Bible reading publication is that it's put together by Christians who believe that by reading the Bible regularly and allowing God to speak through it we can receive the power of God to live like Jesus and do the things he did.

All these titles and many more from SU can be found at your nearest Christian bookshop. Some are available as free samplers for you to try, so if you'd like to do that just write to SU at the address on page 43.

Feedback Welcome!

Scripture Union ☙ SCRIPTURE UNION is a charitable organisation working around the world with the goal of making God's good news known to people of all ages, and encouraging them to meet God regularly through the Bible and prayer. As well as publishing books, Bible reading notes, and a range of church resources, Scripture Union produces videos and audio cassettes, works in schools, and runs holiday clubs and missions for children and young people.

If you'd like to give any feedback about *Bread for the Journey: the Identity series*, or find out more about any aspect of SU, you can:

* log on to http://www.scriptureunion.org.uk
* email info@scriptureunion.org.uk
* telephone 01908 856000
* write to Scripture Union at the address below.

Serving the King of Kings

CPO (Christian Publicity Organisation) is a literature mission, registered charity and professional design, print and distribution service. CPO provides...

* High quality, contemporary church publicity, evangelistic and discipleship resources through a mail order service and e-commerce. For a free catalogue call 01903 266400, or visit our website which has full details of our current catalogue and other services – www.cpo.org.uk

* A design, print and distribution facility that serves the Christian community – from the smallest local church to international charities – with state-of-the-art digital and conventional printing, warehousing and order fulfilment.
  For a free estimate call 01903 264556 and ask for our Print Sales Team. *'Bread for the Journey'* is designed and printed by CPO.

* 'Project Print', a fund supporting literature outreach in developing countries, which subsidises over six million items of print every year. For a leaflet giving further details, call 01903 266400.

If you do not receive regular information about CPO or SU please tick the relevant box below and return this form to the appropriate address.

❏ **Scripture Union**
207-209 Queensway, Bletchley, Milton Keynes. MK2 2EB
Tel: 01908 856000 Fax: 01908 856004
Email: info@scriptureunion.org.uk

❏ **CPO**
Garcia Estate, Canterbury Road, Worthing. BN13 1BW
Tel: 01903 264556 Fax: 01903 830066
Email: info@cpo.org.uk

MORE BREAD FOR THE JOURNEY

If you like what you've read so far, you might like to get the rest of the series. The coupon here will give you 50p off the cost of any of the other titles. Simply take it into your nearest Christian bookshop.

In case of difficulty in getting hold of Bread for the Journey telephone Scripture Union's mail order line on 01908 856006 or CPO on 01903 263354.

Addresses for both are given on page 43.

Who is He ?

Who are you ?

Who are we ?

Bread for the Journey

The Bible
Contemporary English Version

At your local bookshop or order on tel:
0870 900 2050

Who is he?
FREE with the
*CEV Newcomer Bible**

The *CEV Newcomer Bible* has special notes
to help anyone new to Christianity and Bible reading

insights from the Bible

HUNGRY FOR MEANING

- YET STARVED FOR TIME?

BREAD FOR THE JOURNEY

IS FOR YOU!

Bite-sized Bible truths

in a full-colour

magazine format

Scripture
Union

ISBN 1 85999 504 7

CPO
Christian Publicity Organisation

9 781859 995044